STECK-VAUGHN

W9-BCA-288

HEADLINES OF THE CENTURY

1940-1949

Melissa Stone Billings
Henry Billings

STECK-VAUGHN
COMPANY
A Subsidiary of National Education Corporation

Acknowledgments

Executive Editor
Elizabeth Strauss

Project Editor
Kelly Krake

Designer
John Harrison

Electronic Production
Shelly Knapp, Kristian Polo

Photo Editor
Margie Foster

Illustration Credits
David Griffin, p.3

Photo Credits
Cover (inset) American Red Cross.P.5 AP/Wide World; p.6 National Baseball Library, Cooperstown, NY; pp. 7, 8, 9 AP/Wide World; p.13 Culver Pictures; p.14 Courtesy U.S. Navy; pp.15, 16, 17, 21 Culver Pictures; pp. 22, 23 UPI/Bettmann; pp.24, 25 AP/Wide World; p.29 UPI/Bettmann; pp.30, 31 Library of Congress; p.35 Moorland Spingarn Research Center; p.36 AP/Wide World; p.37 The Bettmann Archive; pp.41, 42 UPI/Bettmann; p.43 AP/Wide World; p.47 UPI/Bettmann; p.48 Culver; pp.49, 50, 51 National Baseball Library, Cooperstown, NY; p.55 UPI/Bettmann; p.56 AP/Wide World; p.57 Culver Pictures; pp. 58, 59 UPI/Bettmann; p.63 AP/Wide World; pp.64, 65 UPI/Bettmann; pp.66, 67 AP/Wide World; p.71 UPI/Bettmann; p.72 AP/Wide World; p.73 Courtesy Harry S. Truman Library; pp. 77, 78 UPI/Bettmann; pp.79, 83 AP/Wide World; pp.84, 85 Culver Pictures.

To teacher: This product is reflective of its time. When necessary to the content and understanding of the story, we have chosen to use the names by which ethnic groups were known at that time.

ISBN 0-8114-3294-7

Copyright ©1994 Steck-Vaughn Company. All rights reserved. No part of the material protected by this copyright may be reproduced or utilized in any form or by any means, electronic or mechanical, including photocopying, recording, or by any information storage and retrieval system, without permission in writing from the copyright owner. Requests for permission to make copies of any part of the work should be mailed to: Copyright Permissions, Steck-Vaughn Company, P.O. Box 26015, Austin, TX 78755. Printed in the United States of America.

1 2 3 4 5 6 7 8 9 BP 98 97 96 95 94 93

Headlines of the Century 1940-1949

The years 1940 to 1949 began in war and ended in the fear of war. World War II (1939-1945) brought death to millions of people. Then the Cold War between the United States and the Soviet Union started. Science gave us the jet plane and better medicine. It also gave us nuclear bombs. African Americans were finally allowed to play baseball in the major leagues.

Contents

DIMAGGIO STREAK ENDS

July 18, 1941—The greatest hitting streak in baseball history has ended. For 56 straight games, Joe DiMaggio of the New York Yankees got a hit. Last night he didn't. Twice he came close to getting a hit. But each time, Cleveland third baseman Ken Keltner robbed him of his hit by making a great play. If there is one baseball record that will never be broken, this is it!

DiMaggio gets a home run in the 39th game of his hitting streak.

The Streak Begins

Joe DiMaggio was a terrific baseball player. In fact, he was one of the best ever to play the game. DiMaggio was good at everything. He ran the bases well. He played center field with **style**. He had a powerful throwing arm. And he could hit. Boy, could he ever hit!

Still, no one ever dreamed he would hit in 56 straight games. Certainly no one was thinking that when the **streak** began. The Yankee record for hits was 29 straight games. The major league record, set by George Sisler in 1922, was 41.

DiMaggio's streak began on May 15, 1941. It was a warm, sunny day at Yankee Stadium. The Yankees were playing the Chicago White Sox. Before the game started, Joe DiMaggio was not happy. He had not been hitting well. His **batting average** was just .184 over the past 20 games. Sports writer Max Kase spoke to DiMaggio before the game. "What's wrong, Joe?" he asked. "You haven't been hitting the ball lately."

"I don't know," answered DiMaggio. "I can't seem to get the **rhythm** back in my swing. Maybe today things will change." That day DiMaggio did get a hit. It was nothing special. He got one single in four times at bat. But at least it was a hit. The next day he hit a triple and a home run. A few days later, he went three for three with two singles and a double. "That's more like it," thought DiMaggio.

For the next two months, DiMaggio kept hitting. The streak reached 10 games, then 15. When DiMaggio reached 20, sports reporters and fans began to take notice. By the time his streak passed 30 games, the whole nation was watching.

DiMaggio tried to stay calm. He didn't want to put extra pressure on himself. One day someone asked him if he was keeping count. "No!" he said. "I'm afraid to. Just let me keep hitting. Let somebody else do the counting."

The New York Yankees in 1941

NEW YORK YANKEES
1941

DiMaggio breaks George Sisler's hitting record of 41 games.

It Takes Luck, Too!

Joe DiMaggio was good. There is no question about that. But he was lucky, too. Anyone with a long hitting streak needs a little luck along the way. Luck might be a ground ball that is barely out of reach of an infielder. Or it might be a fly ball that an outfielder can't quite get. In 34 of the 56 games, DiMaggio got only one hit. In any of those 34 games, a great play by the other team would have ended the streak.

DiMaggio got really lucky in game 38. It was the bottom of the eighth inning. The Yankees led the St. Louis Browns by a score of 3 to 1. Joe hadn't gotten a hit all day. There was a good chance he wouldn't get to bat again. He was the fourth batter in line. If the first three batters made outs, the streak would be over. His team wouldn't be up to bat again unless the Browns tied the game or went ahead in the ninth inning.

Yankee batter Johnny Sturns popped out. Then Red Rolfe **walked**. The next Yankee batter was Tommy Henrich. Henrich was known for hitting into **double plays**. If he did that now, it would end the inning and maybe DiMaggio's streak. Henrich didn't want to do that. So he **bunted** the ball. Rolfe moved to second as Henrich was **thrown out** at first.

Joe DiMaggio stepped up to the plate. But would the Browns pitch to him? First base was open. Most teams would have walked a hot hitter like DiMaggio and pitched to the next batter. But again DiMaggio got lucky. The Browns let him hit. On the first pitch, DiMaggio cracked a double into left field. His streak was still hot!

Baseball's Greatest Record

In game 40, DiMaggio faced the Philadelphia Athletics. Their pitcher was Johnny Babich. He was always tough on DiMaggio. Babich would have loved to be the pitcher that broke DiMaggio's streak. In the first inning, he walked DiMaggio. In the fourth, he walked him again. "Babich isn't going to give me any good pitches to hit," DiMaggio thought. "I've been up two times and haven't even swung my bat yet." In the seventh inning, Babich's first pitch was again **high and outside**. This time DiMaggio went after it. He reached up and slapped a single into center field.

DiMaggio hits a single to center field in game 44 of his streak.

DiMaggio gets a single in game 56—the last game of his hitting streak.

The next day the Yankees played two games. In game 41, DiMaggio got a double. That tied Sisler's record. But something happened between games. A fan stole DiMaggio's bat to keep as a **souvenir**. It was Joe's lucky bat. He had used it since his streak began. Now he would have to use a different one. In game 42, DiMaggio was upset about his bat. And he was worried about getting a hit. Three times in a row he hit the ball weakly, each time he made an out. At last in the seventh inning, he got a single to left field. Joe DiMaggio had broken Sisler's record!

DiMaggio now had the greatest hitting streak in history. It became a front-page story. His hits were reported on the radio. People talked about them at home, at work, at school. A special song was written. It was called "Joltin' Joe DiMaggio."

But the streak couldn't last forever. It ended during the 57th game—a night game against the Cleveland Indians. There Ken Keltner took away DiMaggio's two hits with two great plays. In his last time at bat, DiMaggio hit a ground ball to the shortstop who made a double play. The fans knew it was over. They stood and gave Joe DiMaggio one of the longest cheers ever heard in baseball.

Building Vocabulary

■ Match each word with its meaning.

_____ 1. style

_____ 2. rhythm

_____ 3. double play

_____ 4. thrown out

_____ 5. walked

_____ 6. bunted

a. the timing or speed of an action

b. getting two outs in one play

c. arriving at a base after the ball

d. allowed to go to first base after getting four bad pitches

e. tapped the ball a short distance

f. showing beauty and skill

Part B

■ Write the best word or words to complete each sentence. Use each word once.

high and outside	streak	batting average	souvenir

In May of 1941, Joe DiMaggio had a (1) _____ of

.184. Then he went on a hitting (2) _____. He hit all

kinds of pitches, including ones that were (3) _____.

He kept hitting even after someone took his lucky bat as a

(4) _____.

Writing Your Ideas

■ Imagine that you are Joe DiMaggio. On a separate sheet of paper, describe your feelings when your 56-game hitting streak ends.

10

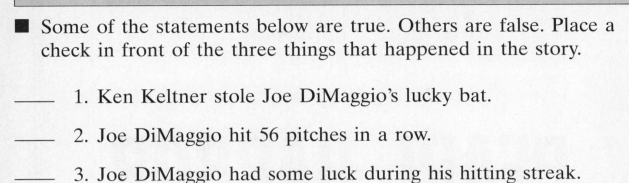

Remembering What You Read

■ Some of the statements below are true. Others are false. Place a check in front of the three things that happened in the story.

_____ 1. Ken Keltner stole Joe DiMaggio's lucky bat.

_____ 2. Joe DiMaggio hit 56 pitches in a row.

_____ 3. Joe DiMaggio had some luck during his hitting streak.

_____ 4. George Sisler broke Joe DiMaggio's record hitting streak.

_____ 5. Joe DiMaggio's streak ended during a game against the Cleveland Indians.

_____ 6. Fans cheered DiMaggio when his hitting streak ended.

Building Skills—Read a Table

■ Use the table to answer the questions about DiMaggio.

	Number of times at bat	Number of Hits	Number of Home Runs
1939	462	176	30
1940	508	179	31
1941	541	193	30
1942	610	186	21

1. In what year did Joe DiMaggio hit the most home runs?_____

_____

2. In what years did Joe DiMaggio get less than 600 times at bat?

_____

3. What was the highest number of hits Joe DiMaggio got?_____

_____

4. How many home runs did Joe DiMaggio hit in 1941?_____

PEARL HARBOR ATTACKED!

December 7, 1941—Enemy planes came out of the sun. At first no one saw them. Then suddenly, at 7:55 A.M., bombs began raining down on Hawaii's Pearl Harbor. The attack caught American soldiers and sailors completely by surprise. Within minutes Japanese planes sank three large ships. They destroyed most U.S. planes before the planes could get off the ground. More than 2,000 Americans are feared dead. Everyone knows what this means. IT MEANS WAR!

War Clouds

By 1940 Japan had taken over part of China. Japan wanted to take over other places in Asia, as well. The United States thought Japan should leave other countries alone. The U.S. held talks with Japan. Both sides hoped to settle their differences without going to war. But the talks went nowhere.

In July 1941, Japan took over Vietnam. This time the United States took action. President Franklin Roosevelt ordered an embargo. An **embargo** meant that the United States would no longer trade with Japan. The Japanese had counted on America for gas, oil, and steel. Now the U.S. would send nothing to Japan.

Roosevelt made another move, as well. He sent American **warships** to Hawaii. "If we end up going to war with Japan, these ships will be ready to go," thought Roosevelt.

The Japanese attack destroyed most U.S. planes before they could get off the ground.

The U.S.S. *Shaw* exploded during the Japanese attack on Pearl Harbor.

There was still a chance to keep peace. New talks were set up between Japan and the United States. Japan was hurt by the embargo. Japanese **officials** asked the U.S. to open trade again. The U.S. said the embargo would end only if Japan ended its war in China. Japan continued to talk about peace but refused to leave China. On November 3, Japanese leaders secretly approved a plan to attack Pearl Harbor.

On November 26, Japanese ships set sail across the Pacific Ocean. They were headed for Hawaii. Japan knew that the United States would win a long war. So Japanese leaders planned to **strike** quickly. "We will strike first, and strike hard," they said to themselves.

The Americans guessed that something was going to happen. But they didn't know what. On November 27, the U.S. government sent a "war warning" to Pearl Harbor. Soldiers and sailors there were told that war could start at any time.

Still, many Americans did not think Japan would attack the United States directly. People thought the attack would come some other place. "The Japanese would not dare strike Pearl Harbor," U.S. leaders thought. "They'll hit the Philippines or Malaysia first. After all, those are the places Japan wants to take over." As everyone soon learned, the U.S. leaders were wrong.

Surprise Attack

The first American to see the Japanese planes was Private Joseph Lockard. He was just learning how to use a **radar** screen. On December 7, around 7:00 A.M., Lockard saw something strange on the screen. He called Lieutenant Kermit Tyler. "Sir," said Lockard, "This is the largest flight of planes I've ever seen."

More than 2,000 Americans died in the attack on Pearl Harbor.

(Left to right) U.S.S. *West Virginia*, U.S.S. *Tennessee*, U.S.S. *Arizona*

The screen showed the first wave of enemy planes. There were 183 planes. They were about 130 miles away. Tyler, too, was young and new to the job. He did not understand what he was seeing. "Some new U.S. planes are coming in from California," he said. "That must be what you're seeing. Don't worry about it," he said.

The Japanese planes closed in. Just before 8:00 A.M., they appeared over Pearl Harbor. The surprise was complete. A band on the U.S.S. *Nevada* was playing the *Star-Spangled Banner* as the American flag was raised. Band members had no idea what was happening. They continued to play even as the first bombs dropped. "This is the best **drill** the Army Air Force has ever put on," one sailor said.

After the war, one officer remembered how he felt when he saw the Japanese planes. "I saw a plane with a big red dot on it. I thought it must be a war game—the reds against the blues." Soon he knew it wasn't a game. "I was scared to death. In four years at sea I sat through 78 air attacks. But nothing was as frightening as the attack on Pearl Harbor."

Pearl Harbor was one of the most one-sided battles in history. On the American side, 2,433 people were killed and another 1,178 wounded. The U.S. also lost 18 ships and 188 planes. Another 159 U.S. planes were damaged. Only about 130 Japanese died in the attack. Japan lost only 29 planes.

A Shocked Nation Reacts

News of the attack **shocked** Americans. At first, no one could believe it. People thought it had to be a mistake. Even some top officials did not believe the news.

Soon people began to face the truth. Their shock turned to pain and anger. They felt pain over the loss of so many Americans. And they felt anger toward the Japanese. They began to call for the United States to strike back at Japan.

On December 8, President Roosevelt asked **Congress** to **declare** war on Japan. His words echoed what most Americans felt. December 7, he said, was "a day which will live in **infamy**."

Wreckage of part of the U.S.S. *Arizona* which was destroyed at Pearl Harbor

Building Vocabulary

■ Read each sentence. Fill in the circle next to the best meaning for the word in dark print. You may use the glossary.

1. President Roosevelt ordered an **embargo**.
   ○ a. decision not to sell things to a country
   ○ b. group of ships to carry supplies   ○ c. war

2. **Warships** were sent to Hawaii.
   ○ a. soldiers   ○ b. hospital supplies   ○ c. ships with guns

3. **Officials** were surprised by the attack on Pearl Harbor.
   ○ a. police officers   ○ b. leaders   ○ c. island people

4. Japan decided to **strike** quickly.
   ○ a. give up   ○ b. attack   ○ c. say they were sorry

5. Joseph Lockard saw something on his **radar** screen.
   ○ a. machine that shows where planes are
   ○ b. book that gives information   ○ c. deadly gas

6. Many sailors thought the attack was a **drill**.
   ○ a. joke   ○ b. mistake   ○ c. practice

7. The attack **shocked** many people.
   ○ a. pleased   ○ b. bored   ○ c. surprised

8. **Congress** acted quickly.
   ○ a. the enemy   ○ b. lawmakers   ○ c. top leader

9. The United States decided to **declare** war.
   ○ a. stay away from   ○ b. announce   ○ c. stop

10. December 7 was a day that would live in **infamy**.
    ○ a. only in America   ○ b. famous for something bad
    ○ c. small children

Writing Your Ideas

■ Imagine that your brother is an American sailor at Pearl Harbor. On a separate sheet of paper, describe how you feel when you first hear about the Japanese attack.

18

Remembering What You Read

■ Fill in the circle next to the best ending for each sentence.

1. The U.S. wanted Japan to
   ○ a. attack Pearl Harbor.   ○ b. leave other countries alone.
   ○ c. sell gas and oil to Americans.

2. On December 7, 1941, Japan attacked
   ○ a. China.   ○ b. Hawaii.   ○ c. New York.

3. Japan attacked Pearl Harbor using
   ○ a. warships.   ○ b. trucks.   ○ c. airplanes.

4. The attack on Pearl Harbor left Americans
   ○ a. happily surprised.   ○ b. angry and upset.
   ○ c. afraid to go to war.

Thinking Critically—Fact or Opinion

■ Write **F** before each fact. Write **O** before each opinion.

_____ 1. The U.S. was wrong to order an embargo.

_____ 2. President Roosevelt should have sent more warships to Pearl Harbor.

_____ 3. Japanese leaders asked the U.S. to end the embargo.

_____ 4. Lieutenant Kermit Tyler should have been punished for the way he read the radar screen.

_____ 5. A "war warning" was sent to Pearl Harbor before the attack.

_____ 6. The Japanese were smart to attack Pearl Harbor instead of the Philippines.

_____ 7. Pearl Harbor was a one-sided battle.

_____ 8. President Roosevelt asked Congress to declare war on Japan.

DOOLITTLE BLASTS TOKYO

May 19, 1942—The secret is out! The United States has bombed Japan! In one of the most daring attacks ever made, U.S. pilots bombed Tokyo and four other Japanese cities. The surprise attack was made on April 18. It was led by Colonel James Doolittle. Doolittle and his men attacked about noon. They blasted factories, ships, and steel mills. The successful attack is the best news from the Pacific since the war began.

Doolittle ties a medal to a bomb in a ceremony on the U.S.S. *Hornet*.

A Daring Leader for a Daring Mission

In early 1942, the United States was still **reeling** from the Japanese attack on Pearl Harbor. Americans wanted to strike back at Japan. But how? Japan controlled most of the Pacific Ocean. Many U.S. warships had been destroyed at Pearl Harbor.

One day General Hap Arnold, head of the Army Air Force, and **Admiral** Ernest King had an idea. What if America bombed Japan? "They caught us by surprise at Pearl Harbor. Let's catch them by surprise in Tokyo," said King.

There was one big problem. How could a **bomber** get to Japan? Japan was too far. No bomber could fly that far from any American air base. Small planes could take off from **aircraft carriers** in the Pacific Ocean. But bombers needed longer **runways**. Still, King and Arnold kept thinking. "It might be possible," they told each other. "We might be able to get our B-25 bombers to take off from aircraft carriers."

It was a long shot. But King and Arnold felt it was worth a try. "This plan must be top secret," they agreed. "If the Japanese hear about it, we will fail for sure. Even if we can surprise them, they may shoot down many of our bombers."

"Who should lead the **mission**?" asked King. Arnold knew right away who he wanted. He picked up his phone. "Get me Doolittle!" he cried.

Jimmy Doolittle was one of the world's great pilots. He was so good that the army hadn't let him fly in World War I battles.

Army leaders were afraid he might get shot down. They thought it was more important that Doolittle live and teach others to fight. After the war, Doolittle set several flying and speed records.

Now Doolittle faced the toughest job of his life. He needed 79 men to help him carry out the plan. He knew they all might die. He asked for **volunteers**. He could not tell them what they would have to do. It was too big a secret. All he could say was that the job would be "**extremely dangerous**." Seventy-nine brave men stepped forward.

B-25 bombers were used on Doolittle's mission.

Doolittle and his men get ready to board their planes on April 18, 1942.

Next, Doolittle and his men worked on the B-25s. They had to make them lighter so they could take off from a short runway. They took out much of the radio **equipment** and most of the guns. They replaced the guns with broomsticks painted black. "Hopefully the Japanese will think we still have guns," he said.

Getting Ready

Doolittle's volunteers trained hard. A B-25 usually needed more than 1,000 feet to take off. On an aircraft carrier it would have less than half that much. The pilots practiced on fields marked with flags. They raced their engines, then roared quickly down the field. Slowly they learned how to take off in less than 500 feet.

On April 2, the men boarded the aircraft carrier *Hornet*. Only then did Doolittle tell them what their mission was. The plan was simple. On April 19, the *Hornet* would be 450 miles from Japan. Doolittle and the others would climb into 16 planes. They would fly across the Pacific and drop their bombs over Japanese cities at night. Then they would fly to China and hope for the best.

The Attack

But early on the morning of April 18, something went wrong. A Japanese ship spotted the *Hornet*.

"The plan has been changed," Doolittle told his men. "Now that we've been seen, the Japanese army will soon figure out what we're doing. We have to attack right away. Good luck, men!"

So at 8:20 A.M. on April 18, Doolittle's plane took off. One by one, the other B-25s followed. All the practice had paid off. None of the pilots had trouble with the short runway.

The mission went smoothly. The Japanese could not believe they were being bombed. They were too surprised to shoot down any of the B-25s.

Doolittle's plane is the first to leave the *Hornet*.

These eight members of Doolittle's mission were photographed in China after their successful attack on Japan.

Still, the 80 Americans faced great danger. As they headed into China, they were low on **fuel**. It was dark and cloudy. The men knew only that they were somewhere over China or the China Sea. As fuel ran out, they had to jump from their planes or crash land. Most, including Doolittle, jumped.

Doolittle landed in a rice field. He did not know what had happened to the 79 other men or their planes. He feared most had been shot down. He felt sure the mission had failed. But Doolittle was wrong. The attack was a success. Over the next month, most of the men made their way back from China. Only eight were captured by the enemy.

Doolittle's actions made him a hero and a general. President Franklin Roosevelt gave him the Medal of Honor. *The New York Daily News* said what many were thinking. "Doolittle," it wrote, "should be named *Doomuch.*"

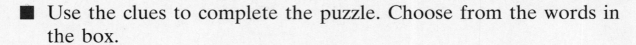
■ Use the clues to complete the puzzle. Choose from the words in the box.

aircraft carriers
volunteers
mission
equipment
runways
admiral
reeling
fuel
extremely
bomber

Across

2. an important job

4. a plane that carries bombs

6. ships that carry airplanes

9. airplanes take off and land on these

10. motors need this to run

Down

1. people who offer to help

3. tools needed to do something

5. very

7. top navy officer

8. spinning from a surprise

Writing Your Ideas

■ Imagine that you are one of the 79 volunteers. Write how you felt when you first found out what your secret mission would be.

Remembering What You Read

■ Answer the questions.

1. Who led the bombing mission?_____

2. Why was it hard for bombers to take off from aircraft carriers?

   _____

3. Why did the men take radio equipment and guns off their B-25s?

   _____

4. Where did the men fly after dropping their bombs?_____

   _____

Building Skills—Read a Graph

■ Use the graph to answer the questions. Each soldier represents 25,000 deaths.

Total Number of Americans Who Died in Battle
American Revolution
Civil War
World War I
World War II
Korean War
Vietnam

1. In what war did the fewest number of Americans die in battle?

   _____

2. In what war did the most Americans die in battle?_____

3. Did more Americans die in battle during the Civil War or

   World War I?_____

4. Does the graph show how many Americans died in battle during

   the Korean War?_____

LENDING A HELPING HAND

July 23, 1942—It's a deal! Today the United States and Mexico signed an agreement that will bring thousands of Mexican workers to the United States. This deal has come just in time. Harvest season is only a few weeks away. American farmers need help. Many American men are overseas fighting World War II. There are not enough U.S. workers to pick the crops. Luckily, Mexican workers are stepping in to help.

Helping to Win the War

The real name of the deal was the Mexican Farm **Labor** Supply Program. Most people just called it the "Braceros Program." Braceros is a Spanish word meaning hired hand. When it was announced in July 1942, American farmers were happy. They agreed to pay the Mexican workers fair **wages**. They also promised to give them **decent** places to live. In return, the workers agreed to work 8 to 12 hours a day harvesting crops.

It seemed like a good deal for both sides. American farmers would get the help they needed. And Mexicans would get better jobs than they could find back home. The program was good in another way, as well. Like the United States, Mexico had declared war on Germany and Japan. But Mexico did not have much of an army. Harvesting crops was one way Mexicans could help with the war **effort**.

Mexican farm workers enter the U.S. to pick crops.

These farm workers are loading a truck with sugar beets.

A Good Start

At first, the Braceros Program was a big success. Thousands of Mexicans volunteered for the program. On September 29, the first 500 workers arrived in California. They were given a warm welcome. Farmers cheered their arrival. A band played. A **banquet** of fine food was served.

Soon more Mexicans arrived. Americans tried to make them feel at home. Radio stations ran programs in Spanish. Newspapers ran stories thanking the workers for being good neighbors. "They're **courteous**, **considerate**, and good workers," said one farmer. Others agreed.

Problems Develop

To some, the Braceros Program seemed perfect. But there were problems. For one thing, the Mexicans missed their homes. Many had young wives and children in Mexico. It was true they made more money in the U.S., but many were very **homesick**.

As time passed, other problems came up. Some Mexicans found they were not treated well. The "houses" that farmers offered them were too **run-down** to live in. Some workers were **discriminated** against because they were Hispanic. Farmers back in Mexico complained, too. They said the best workers left for America just when Mexican crops needed to be picked.

But for better or worse, the Braceros Program kept running.

By 1947, almost 250,000 Mexicans had come to America. Many worked on farms. The rest worked on railroads. Between 1948 and 1964, the numbers were even higher. Four and a half million Mexican workers came during this time. At last, in 1964, the Braceros Program ended.

In spite of the problems, the program had done many good things. Perhaps the most important thing it did was to teach Mexicans and Americans more about each other.

Farm workers in the lettuce fields

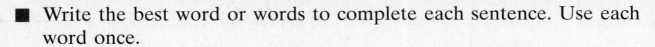

Building Vocabulary

■ Write the best word or words to complete each sentence. Use each word once.

| discriminated | run-down | homesick | effort | wages |
| considerate | banquet | Labor | decent | courteous |

1. _____ means thoughtful of others.

2. The Mexican Farm _____ Supply Program was called the Braceros Program.

3. Some workers were given _____ houses.

4. Mexico wanted to help with the war _____.

5. Many Americans _____ against Hispanic people.

6. Farmers promised the workers _____ housing.

7. Many Mexican workers became _____.

8. Farmers greeted the workers with a _____ of fine food.

9. Farmers agreed to pay the workers fair _____.

10. The Mexican farm workers were _____.

Writing Your Ideas

■ Imagine that you are a Mexican worker in America in the 1940s. Write a letter back home describing your life in America.

Remembering What You Read

■ Some of the statements below are true. Others are false. Place a check in front of the three things that happened in the story.

_____ 1. Mexico declared war on the United States.

_____ 2. Mexican workers helped gather American crops.

_____ 3. American farmers welcomed Mexican workers.

_____ 4. Mexican workers missed their homes.

_____ 5. Mexicans were not good workers.

_____ 6. The Braceros Program ended after only six months.

Thinking Critically—Cause and Effect

■ Complete the following sentences.

1. There were not enough Americans to harvest crops because_____

_____

2. Mexican workers were willing to come to America because_____

_____

3. American radio stations ran programs in Spanish because_____

_____

4. Mexican workers were unhappy with their housing because_____

_____

5. Mexico wanted to help with the war effort because_____

_____

BLOOD BREAKTHROUGH

March 31, 1944—Thank you, Dr. Drew! These were the words everyone kept repeating yesterday. Dr. Charles Richard Drew was being honored for the work he did during World War II. Drew found a way to get blood to thousands of people who had been injured. Without this blood, more people would surely have died. Dr. Drew's work has made him a hero to millions.

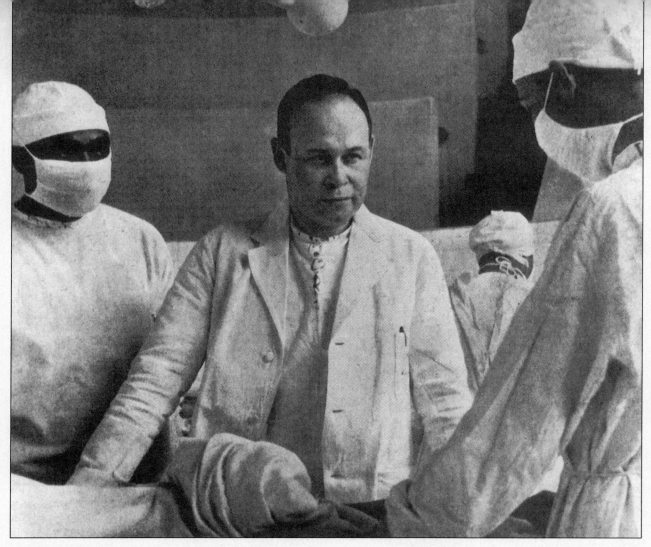

Dr. Charles Drew's work with blood helped many patients who had surgery.

What to Do?

As a child, Charles Drew wanted to ride race horses. He was disappointed when he grew too big to be a **jockey**. "I guess I'll have to find something else to do with my life," he thought.

In 1922 he finished high school in Washington, D.C. He wanted to go to **college**. But his family did not have much money. Besides, many colleges did not want African American students. Luckily Amherst College in Massachusetts was different. Amherst College offered Drew a **scholarship**. Drew worked hard at Amherst. He wanted to become a doctor.

In 1928 Drew entered McGill University's school of medicine in Canada. Drew loved medical school. He began working with Dr. John Beattie. Beattie was doing studies on blood. After Beattie went home to England, Drew continued studying blood on his own.

Working with Plasma

Before the 1930s, many people died from loss of blood after injuries. **Researchers** found that a person's blood could be replaced with blood from another person. People could **donate** blood to those who needed it. But the donated blood had to be used right away. Blood did not stay fresh long.

Drew looked for a way to make blood last longer. He and other doctors began experimenting with **plasma**. Plasma is the liquid part of blood that holds the red blood cells. Drew and others found that plasma could be stored for long periods of time. Plasma could be used in **transfusions** in place of whole blood. Plasma could be stored for **emergencies**.

This important news came just in time. In 1940 Germany bombed Great Britain. Many British men, women, and children were hurt. These people needed blood. Whole blood did not stay fresh long enough to reach them. Plasma was needed. But no **system** had been set up for using plasma.

In 1944 Dr. Drew was awarded the Spingarn Medal.

American Red Cross Bloodmobile delivers blood plasma to a hospital.

Then John Beattie, who was in Great Britain, had an idea. "Dr. Drew knows as much about blood as anyone else in the world. Maybe he can set up a system for us."

A Hero

Charles Drew agreed to help. He had already set up a blood bank in the hospital where he worked. He got other New York City hospitals to do the same thing. He asked Americans to donate blood to the blood banks.

The plasma was separated out of the blood. Then the plasma was dried and sent to England.

Drew's work made him a hero in Britain. In 1941 he helped the United States set up its own system for using plasma. In 1944 Drew won the Spingarn Medal. This medal is given for the highest **achievement** by an African American during the last year. Dr. Drew's work with plasma had saved thousands of lives and changed the world of medicine.

Building Vocabulary

■ Match each word with its meaning.

_____ 1. scholarship
_____ 2. plasma
_____ 3. transfusions
_____ 4. system
_____ 5. jockey
_____ 6. researchers
_____ 7. emergencies
_____ 8. achievement
_____ 9. donate
_____ 10. college

a. the liquid part of blood

b. a planned way of doing things

c. person who rides horses in races

d. people who study things carefully

e. something worthwhile you have done

f. give

g. events that call for fast action

h. putting blood from one person into another person

i. money given to pay for schooling

j. a school of further learning which some people go to after high school

Writing Your Ideas

■ Imagine that you are in charge of a blood bank. On a separate sheet of paper, write an advertisement to get people to give blood.

Remembering What You Read

■ Fill in the circle next to the best ending for each sentence.

1. Charles Drew was a
   ○ a. doctor.   ○ b. soldier.   ○ c. banker.

2. Charles Drew spent years working with
   ○ a. lungs.   ○ b. blood.   ○ c. bombs.

3. Charles Drew first became a hero in
   ○ a. Great Britain.   ○ b. Russia.   ○ c. Germany.

4. Charles Drew saved thousands of lives during
   ○ a. World War I.   ○ b. World War II.
   ○ c. the Korean War.

Building Skills—Use a Diagram

■ Use the diagram to answer the questions.

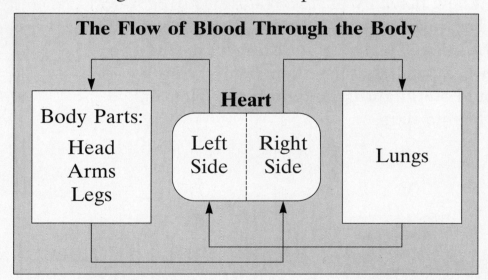

The Flow of Blood Through the Body

Body Parts: Head Arms Legs — Heart Left Side | Right Side — Lungs

1. Where does blood go after it leaves the lungs?_____

2. Where does blood go after leaving the left side of the heart?

   _____

3. Which side of the heart sends blood to the lungs?_____

4. What are the two sides of the heart?_____

TOKYO ROSE ARRESTED

September 8, 1945—The police found "Tokyo Rose" today! Her real name is Iva Toguri. But American soldiers know her only as Tokyo Rose. During World War II, her voice was often heard on Japanese radio. She talked sweetly about life in America. She tried to make U.S. soldiers miss their homes. She hoped they would stop fighting and go home. Now Tokyo Rose is behind bars.

An American "Tokyo Rose"

Iva Toguri was not the only "Tokyo Rose." As least ten other women played the part. They all spoke perfect English. But the other "Tokyo Roses" grew up in Japan. Toguri was born and raised in Los Angeles. She was an American **citizen**.

On July 5, 1941, Toguri went to Japan to visit a sick aunt. The United States and Japan were not at war then, so it didn't seem like a dangerous thing to do. While she was there, war broke out between the two countries. Toguri found herself trapped in Japan.

A Prisoner of War?

Toguri tried to make the best of it. She became a secretary for Radio Tokyo. Then, because she spoke English, she was picked to talk on the radio. She was told to say things to make American soldiers homesick. She was told to break their spirits.

Iva Toguri is led to her jail cell in October 1945.

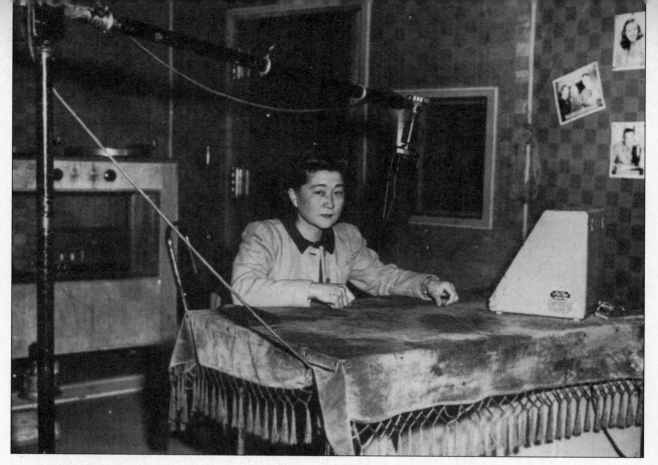

Iva Toguri seated behind the microphone she used to broadcast programs to U.S. soldiers

Toguri called herself "**Orphan Annie**" because she felt she had lost her home. Soldiers who heard her gave her a different name. They called her Tokyo Rose. It was true that these men missed their homes. But Toguri did not get them to stop fighting. She did not break their spirits. Most soldiers simply found Tokyo Rose funny. They listened to her whenever they could.

Fighting for the Truth

Six days after the war ended, U.S. army police **arrested** Tokyo Rose in Japan. They were angry that she had tried to **influence** American soldiers. They thought Tokyo Rose should be punished. Toguri confessed that she had made the **broadcasts**. But she explained that she had felt like a prisoner during the war. No one believed her.

In 1949 Toguri was brought to the United States for **trial**. She was charged with **treason**. The case against her rested on one radio statement she had made. She had said to soldiers, "Orphans of the Pacific, you are really orphans now. How will you get home now that your ships are sunk?"

It was a lie. No ships had been sunk. Some people said this proved Toguri was a **traitor**. It proved she was trying to make American soldiers give up. The court agreed. On October 6, 1949, Toguri was found **guilty** of turning against her own country. She was the first American woman ever found guilty of treason.

Toguri spent six and one-half years in prison and had to pay $10,000. She lost her right to be an American citizen. Still, she kept saying she was not guilty. "America is my home," she said. "It will always be my home. I never did anything to hurt the country I love."

Slowly she won people over to her side. On January 19, 1977, President Gerald Ford **pardoned** her. At the age of 60, Iva Toguri finally became an American citizen again.

This photograph of Iva Toguri was taken shortly before her 1949 trial for treason.

Building Vocabulary

Part A

■ Write the best word to complete each sentence. Use each word once.

treason	broadcasts	pardoned	guilty

Iva Toguri made radio (1)_____ to soldiers

during World War II. After the war, she was charged with

(2)_____. She was found (3)_____.

Later, however, she was (4)_____.

Part B

■ Match each word with its meaning.

_____ 1. orphan

_____ 2. arrested

_____ 3. traitor

_____ 4. citizen

_____ 5. trial

_____ 6. influence

a. picked up and held by police

b. person who is part of a country

c. person who turns against his or her own country

d. court test to see if someone has broken a law

e. cause someone to change his or her actions or feelings

f. person whose parents are dead

Writing Your Ideas

■ Imagine that you are a soldier listening to Tokyo Rose. On a separate sheet of paper, describe how you feel about her.

Remembering What You Read

■ Answer the questions.

1. Why did Iva Toguri go to Japan in 1941?_____

_____

2. What did the "Tokyo Roses" try to do during their broadcasts?

_____

_____

3. How did most soldiers feel about Tokyo Rose?_____

_____

4. What happened to Iva Toguri after World War II ended?_____

_____

_____

Thinking Critically—Sequence

■ Number the sentences to show the order in which things happened in the story. The first one is done for you.

_____ Iva Toguri was pardoned by President Ford.

__1__ Iva Toguri went to Japan to visit a sick aunt.

_____ U.S. army police arrested Iva Toguri.

_____ Iva Toguri was found guilty of treason.

_____ Iva Toguri became "Tokyo Rose."

JACKIE ROBINSON JOINS DODGERS!

April 11, 1947—There is a new player in major league baseball! His name is Jackie Robinson. Today the Brooklyn Dodgers made Robinson part of their team. He is expected to be in the starting line-up when the season opens next week. Reports say Robinson is a strong hitter. They also say he has great speed. But that's not why he is making headlines. The biggest news of all is that Jackie Robinson is not white.

Jackie Robinson and Branch Rickey

Becoming a Dodger

In 1947 most major league baseball players were white. Some were Hispanic. A few were Native American. But none were African American. Many African Americans were good enough players to be major league stars. But whites discriminated against African Americans in many areas. Baseball was one.

In 1946 Branch Rickey started to change that. Rickey was the president of the Brooklyn Dodgers. He wanted to make the Dodgers a stronger team. Rickey decided to sign up African American players. "It's time some of these men played for the Dodgers!" he said to himself. "They could help us win ball games."

Rickey was interested in a 27-year-old African American named Jackie Robinson. Robinson was a wonderful **athlete**. In college he had been a star in football and basketball. Rickey asked Robinson if he wanted to play for the Dodgers. Rickey said he could start with their **minor league** team in Canada. If he was good enough, Jackie could come to Brooklyn to play with the Dodgers. Robinson was surprised. He never thought the major league would be opened to him.

Rickey warned Robinson that it would not be easy. Many white players would be against him. Fans and players both would be mean to him. "I want a ballplayer with guts enough not to fight back!" Rickey said. "You've got to do this job with base hits and stolen bases and **fielding** ground balls, Jackie. Nothing else!"

Robinson understood. He would have to be careful not to lose his temper or get into fights. He could not give fans any excuses to complain about him. After thinking it over, Robinson accepted Rickey's offer. He spent the 1946 season in Canada. On April 11, 1947, he was offered a **contract** to play in the majors. He signed it without even looking to see what he would be paid.

Proving Himself

Opening day of the 1947 season was April 15. It was a cold, cloudy day in Brooklyn. The Dodgers played the Boston Braves. Jackie Robinson was nervous. He knew he was as good as the white players. At last he had the chance to prove it. Millions of African Americans were praying he would **succeed**.

As the first African American in the major leagues, Robinson was the target of much hatred.

48

Robinson was eager to prove that he belonged in the major leagues.

His first time at bat, Robinson grounded out. He failed to get a hit in his next two tries. His worst moment came in his fourth time at bat. He hit into a double play. The Dodgers won the game, but Robinson went home without a hit.

Over the next few games, Robinson loosened up a bit. He stopped swinging at bad pitches. He began to hit the ball hard. As his hitting got stronger, he showed that he was also a good base runner. He liked to take big **leads**. As one sports writer said, "Robinson dances and prances off base, keeping the enemy upset and off balance, and worrying the pitcher." In his first season, Robinson stole 26 bases. This was more than any other National League player. Twice that year Robinson did the hardest thing a base runner can do—he stole home.

Dealing with Hate

Clearly Robinson had the skill to be a Brooklyn Dodger. Even so, some people wanted him out of the majors. These people thought baseball should remain a white sport. They booed Robinson when he ran out on the field. They called him terrible names and wrote him angry letters.

Players, too, were cruel to Robinson. Some of his own teammates wrote to Branch Rickey saying they wanted Robinson off the team. Players on other teams often yelled at Robinson. Some refused to shake his hand. Some tried to cut him with the spikes on their shoes.

Robinson knew that these people hated him because he was African American. He knew it was unfair. And he was angry about it. But he remembered what Rickey had told him. He could not afford to fight back. "I'd get mad," Robinson later said. "But I'd never let them know it."

Every day seemed to bring some new **insult**. Restaurants refused to serve Robinson. Hotels would not let him check in. Several times he received death **threats**. It took a lot of **courage** to face such hate every day. But Robinson said, "Anybody who says I can't make it doesn't know what I've gone through and what I'm prepared to go through to stay in the majors."

Jackie Robinson poses in his Dodgers uniform.

50

The 1949 Brooklyn Dodgers

Slowly things did get a little better. Robinson's teammates saw how tough it was for him. They saw how well he handled himself. They also saw that he was helping them win ball games. Soon they started treating him better. A few, like Pee Wee Reese, were openly friendly. By September a group of Dodgers came to Robinson. They told him they were behind him 100 per cent.

The same sort of thing was happening all across the country. Whites were learning to admire Jackie Robinson. In the fall of 1947, he was named **Rookie** of the Year.

Jackie Robinson went on to play ten years in the majors. Every year he faced some trouble. But he helped prove that African Americans belonged in major league baseball. Jackie Robinson showed the world that he was a great ballplayer and a great man.

Building Vocabulary

■ Use the clues to complete the puzzle. Choose from words in the box.

| minor league |
| leads |
| succeed |
| insults |
| courage |
| rookie |
| athlete |
| fielding |
| contracts |
| threats |

Across

2. mean, hurtful words
7. player in his first year
8. person who plays sports well
9. do well at something
10. heading toward a base before the pitch is made

Down

1. group of teams where players get ready for major leagues
3. statements that something bad will happen to you
4. agreements between two people
5. catching or picking up a ball that has been hit
6. brave feelings

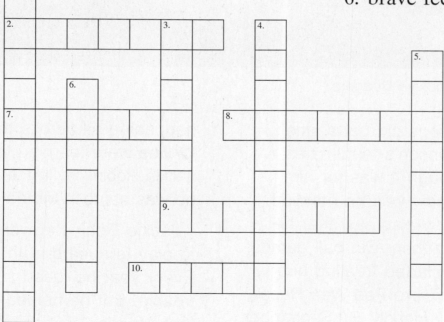

Writing Your Ideas

■ Imagine that you are Jackie Robinson. On a separate sheet of paper, describe how you feel when fans boo you and call you names.

Remembering What You Read

■ Fill in the circle next to the best ending for each sentence.

1. Jackie Robinson played for the
   ○ a. Boston Braves.   ○ b. Brooklyn Dodgers.
   ○ c. New York Yankees.

2. Jackie Robinson was a great
   ○ a. base runner.   ○ b. pitcher.   ○ c. manager.

3. Some people were mean to Jackie Robinson because he was
   ○ a. old.   ○ b. Hispanic.   ○ c. African American.

4. In his first year in the majors, Jackie Robinson faced a lot of
   ○ a. laughs.   ○ b. hate.   ○ c. kindness.

Building Skills—Use a Time Line

■ Use the time line to answer the questions.

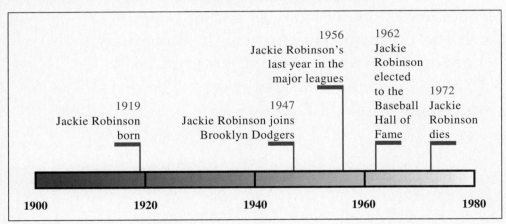

1. When did Jackie Robinson leave the major leagues?_____

2. Is Jackie Robinson still alive?_____

3. In what year was Jackie Robinson born?_____

4. What happened to Jackie Robinson in 1962?_____

_____

TRAGIC STORY TOLD

July 1, 1947—Last month a small book began appearing in bookstores in Holland. Its cover looks quite ordinary. But its pages contain an amazing story. The story is one of sadness and of hope. It will touch the hearts of all who read it. Some may find it hard to believe that such a powerful book was written by a young girl. But it was. The girl's name was Anne Frank.

Frightening News

Anne Frank was born in Germany in 1929. When she was three years old, the Nazis came to power in her country. This was bad news for the Franks. Anne and her family were Jewish. Nazi leader Adolf Hitler hated Jews.

The Franks moved to Holland in 1933. They hoped that there they would be safe from the Nazis. But in 1940, Hitler took over Holland. The Franks found themselves trapped in a Nazi state.

By this time, Adolf Hitler had developed an **evil** plan. He wanted to round up all Jews and kill them. Nazi police began doing this. They rounded up hundreds of thousands of Jews all over Europe. They took men, women, old people, babies—every Jew they could find. These people were sent to special prisons called **concentration camps**. Jews were forced to do hard labor. They were given very little food. Every week thousands were shot or killed in **gas chambers**.

Anne Frank was 13 years old when this photograph was taken.

Dit is een foto, zoals ik me zou wensen, altijd zo te zijn. Dan had ik nog wel een kans om naar Holywood te komen.

Anne Frank.
10 Oct. 1942

(translation)
"This is a photo as I would wish myself to look all the time. Then I would maybe have a chance to come to Hollywood."
Anne Frank, 10 Oct. 1942

This is the building in Amsterdam where Anne and her family lived in hiding for two years.

Anne's father, Otto, hoped to save his family from the Nazis. He began preparing secret rooms above his office. "If necessary," he thought, "we can hide there."

On July 5, 1942, the Franks heard frightening news. The Nazis were looking for Anne's 16-year-old sister, Margot. They were coming to take her to a concentration camp.

The Franks hurried to the hiding place above Otto's office. Otto's business partner, Mr. Van Daan, and his wife and son joined them. So did a friend named Albert Dussel. Together these eight people settled into their "secret annex." They stayed there for two years. Anne spent much of the time writing in her diary. It was this diary that came out as a book in June 1947.

Words of Pain and Hope

Anne used her diary to record her thoughts about her family. She wrote about how much she loved her father. She told about fights with her sister. Sometimes Anne wrote about her old friends. She missed them. She missed her home, her school, and her old life. She wished she could go outside again. "I long for freedom and fresh air . . ." she wrote.

Anne also described the fights that broke out among the eight people in the annex. "Why do grown-ups **quarrel** so easily, so much, and over the most **idiotic** things?" she wrote one day.

Actually, it is easy to understand why these people lost their temper. They were **tense** and worried. They knew their lives were in danger. The waiting never seemed to end. Anne sometimes became **depressed**. One day she wrote in her diary, "Don't **condemn** me; remember that sometimes I too can reach the bursting point."

Life inside the annex certainly was hard. But they all knew it was harder outside. In October 1942, Anne wrote, "Our many Jewish friends are being taken away by the dozen. These people are being loaded into cattle trucks and sent to a camp . . ." Three months later she wrote, "It is terrible outside. Day and night more of those poor people are being dragged off. Families are torn apart. Children coming home from school find that their parents have disappeared. Women return from shopping to find their homes shut up and their families gone."

Anne Frank

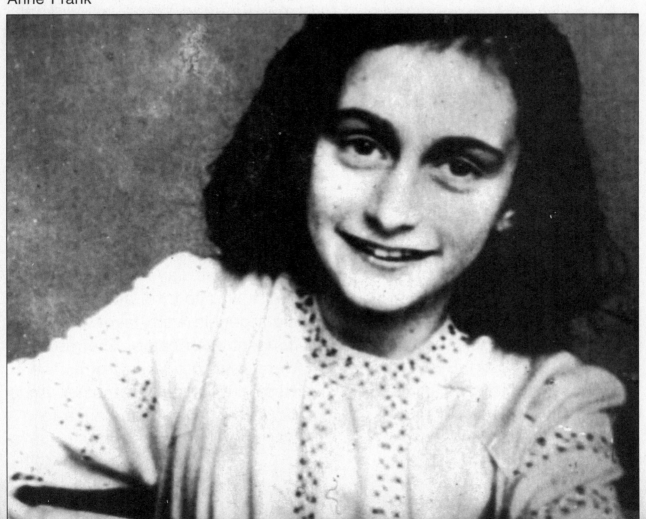

On the 50th anniversary of Anne's birth, her father shows the family's hiding place to Queen Juliana of the Netherlands.

At times Anne felt she was losing hope. After 16 months in hiding, she wrote, "I simply can't imagine that the world will ever be normal again. I do talk about after the war, but then it is only a castle in the air, something that will never really happen."

Somehow, though, Anne did keep her hope alive. By 1944, she even found herself falling in love with 17-year-old Peter Van Daan. Her writings show how uncertain and excited she was about this.

Anne Frank's Words Live On

Anne Frank wrote in her diary for the last time on August 1, 1944. Three days later, five Nazi police stormed the annex. All eight people were taken to a concentration camp. The men were sent to one part of it. The women were sent to another. Anne never even had the chance to say good-by to her father.

In the camp, Anne's mother soon died of **exhaustion**. Anne and her sister were healthier. But by early 1945, they were both very weak. A friend who saw Anne there said she was hungry and sick. Margot died in March, 1945. A few days later, Anne died of hunger and illness.

Otto Frank was the only one of the eight who managed to stay alive. When the war ended, he went back to Holland. He hoped to find his wife and daughters there. Instead, he found Anne's diary.

Otto Frank decided to share the diary with the world. He wanted people to know what a brave, beautiful girl Anne had been. At first the book came out in Dutch. It was called *The Secret Annex*. Later it came out in English as *The Diary of a Young Girl*.

Since 1947 the book has been printed in 30 languages. People today are still deeply touched by Anne Frank's spirit. Anne knew the Nazis wanted to kill her and her family just because they were Jewish. Yet she wrote that "In spite of everything, I still believe that people are really good at heart."

Adolf Hitler

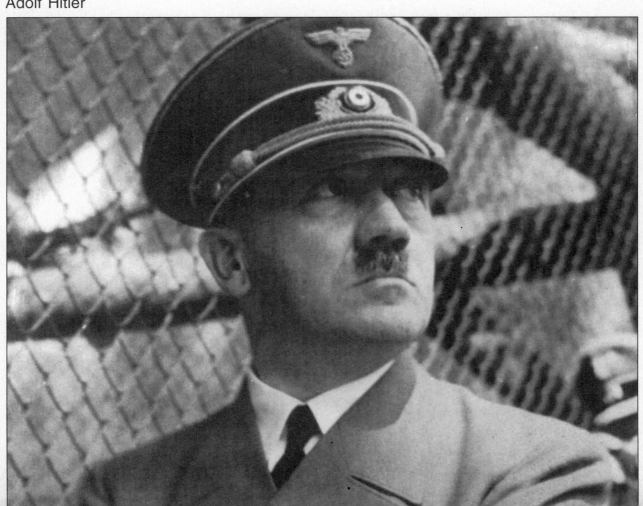

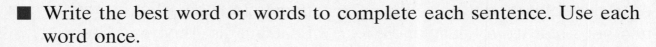

Building Vocabulary

■ Write the best word or words to complete each sentence. Use each word once.

gas chambers	annex	concentration camps	idiotic
tense	quarrel	condemn	exhaustion
evil	depressed		

1. Anne thought the fights that broke out were _____.

2. The Franks hid in a "secret _____."

3. Nazis took Jews to _____ _____.

4. Anne wondered why grown-ups _____ so easily.

5. Anne's family often felt _____.

6. Anne's mother died of _____.

7. Many Jews were killed in _____ _____.

8. Adolf Hitler and his Nazis were _____.

9. In her diary, Anne wrote "Don't _____ me."

10. Sometimes Anne felt _____.

Writing Your Ideas

■ Imagine that you are Anne Frank's father. On a separate sheet of paper, describe how you feel when you find Anne's diary.

Remembering What You Read

■ Some of the statements below are true. Others are false. Place a check in front of the three things that happened in the story.

_____ 1. The Franks hid from the Nazis for two years.

_____ 2. Anne Frank became a member of the Nazis.

_____ 3. Anne Frank died in a concentration camp.

_____ 4. Anne Frank kept a diary during her years in hiding.

_____ 5. Anne Frank's father showed the Nazis where Anne was hiding.

_____ 6. Anne Frank married Peter Van Daan after the war ended.

Thinking Critically—Conclusions

■ Finish each sentence by writing the best answer.

1. The Nazis wanted to kill the Franks because _____

_____

2. The Franks moved to Holland because _____

_____

3. The Franks could not leave their secret annex because _____

_____

4. Anne stopped writing in her diary because _____

_____

5. Otto Frank returned to Holland after the war because _____

_____

SOUND BARRIER BROKEN!

October 14, 1947—Can a plane go faster than the speed of sound? Chuck Yeager answered that question today. At an Air Force base in California, Captain Yeager became the first person ever to fly faster than the speed of sound. He did it in a special plane called the Bell X-1. Using the plane's special rockets, he managed to go faster than 662 miles an hour.

By the age of 25, Chuck Yeager had flown faster than the speed of sound several times.

A Brave Man

Some pilots thought that breaking the sound **barrier** meant certain death. But Charles "Chuck" Yeager had **risked** his life before. During World War II, he was an American fighter pilot based in England. In 1944 he was shot down over Germany. Despite a leg **wound**, he made his way to France. He tried to get to England by slipping through Spain. The Spanish police caught him and put him in jail. He broke out by using a saw to cut through the bars. Soon Yeager was back in England, flying again. By the end of the war, he had shot down 13 German planes.

After the war, Yeager became a great test pilot. He did not seem to be afraid of anything. He would run any test the **engineers** wanted. "He's the coolest guy I've ever seen," said engineer Richard Frost. "He flies a plane as though it were part of him. In his test work he does exactly what the engineers want. Then he brings back the answers."

In 1947 airplane engineers were very interested in the "sound barrier." No one was even sure such a thing **existed**. But many believed it did. Engineers thought this barrier made it **physically** impossible to travel faster than sound. (The speed of sound is about 662 miles an hour.)

Test pilots reported that scary things happened whenever they came close to the speed of sound. **Shock waves** rocked the plane. Shock waves were caused by air rushing over and under the plane's wings. The shock waves were very powerful. They could tear a plane to bits. They sometimes made it impossible to keep a plane on course. "I completely lost control of my plane," said one test pilot. "It started spinning toward the ground. I was lucky to **regain** control just in time."

Chuck Yeager standing beside the Bell X-1

The Bell X-1 in flight

Stories like this made some pilots nervous. They didn't want to run any more tests on the sound barrier. Pilots felt the danger was just too great. Chuck Yeager disagreed. Yeager did not believe in the barrier. He was happy when the Air Force picked him to run tests on the sound barrier. Yeager believed a plane *could* go faster than 662 miles an hour. He suspected that when it did, the shock waves would disappear and the plane again would fly smoothly. But could Yeager really go faster than sound and come back to tell about it? "I'll be back all right," he said with a grin. "In one piece or a whole lot of little pieces."

The Bell X-1

A special plane was needed to **challenge** the sound barrier. No regular plane could do the job. The new plane had to be strong enough to hold together at great speeds. It also had to have a very powerful motor. The Air Force asked the Bell Aircraft company to build such a plane. In 1945 the company began to work on it. They called the plane the Bell X-1.

The Bell X-1 was a small, fat-looking plane. It was shaped like a bullet. The plane had a special rocket motor that gave it plenty of power. But the plane could carry only two and a half minutes' of fuel. The Bell X-1 couldn't take off like other planes. A normal takeoff would use too much fuel.

The builders had to find another way to get the Bell X-1 into the air. "Why not hook it under a large plane like the B-29?" they asked each other. "The B-29 could carry it up to 26,000 feet, then just drop it. At that point, the test pilot could fire the rocket motor and fly away."

The Air Force agreed to try the plan. Twenty-one times the Bell X-1 was carried into the air by a B-29. Twenty-one times a practice drop was made. Each test was a success. At last, the Air Force was ready for Yeager to make the biggest test of all.

Breaking the Sound Barrier

On October 14, 1947, Yeager took off aboard a B-29. Hooked to the belly of this big plane was the Bell X-1. At 7,000 feet, Yeager climbed down a ladder to the Bell X-1. He squeezed through a door in its side. There was barely enough room inside for even a small man like himself.

Yeager is congratulated by the president of the Bell Aircraft Corporation after breaking another speed record in 1953.

Yeager at a press conference after the flight

The B-29 climbed to 26,000 feet. Major Robert Cardenas, the pilot of the B-29, called to Yeager. "One minute warning."

Yeager later admitted that he was scared as he watched the seconds tick off his clock. Then Cardenas spoke again. "Three. . . two. . . one. . . Drop!"

The B-29 dropped the Bell X-1 as if it were a bomb. Yeager fired his rocket motor. The Bell X-1 flashed through the sky. The full power of the plane surprised even Yeager. It pinned him back against his seat. "It was like having hold of something by the tail," he later said, "but not daring to let go."

As Yeager approached the speed of sound, the Bell X-1 started to shake. Then, suddenly, the shaking stopped. Yeager had been right! On the other side of the sound barrier, there were no shock waves! The Bell X-1 flew beautifully as it reached 700 miles per hour.

After two and one-half minutes, Yeager was out of fuel. He glided the plane toward Earth. Seven minutes later, he was safely on the ground. Chuck Yeager was still in one piece. But the sound barrier had been **shattered** forever.

Building Vocabulary

■ Read each sentence. Fill in the circle next to the best meaning for the word in dark print. You may use the glossary.

1. Chuck Yeager wanted to break the sound **barrier**.
   ○ a. building   ○ b. something that blocks
   ○ c. long, thin bar

2. He had **risked** his life before.
   ○ a. taken a chance with   ○ b. ruined   ○ c. enjoyed

3. He had a leg **wound**.
   ○ a. bandage   ○ b. cut   ○ c. decoration

4. He ran any test the **engineers** wanted.
   ○ a. pilots   ○ b. people who design machines
   ○ c. people in restaurants

5. No one was sure the sound barrier **existed**.
   ○ a. went away   ○ b. was strong   ○ c. was real

6. Some thought Yeager's job was **physically** impossible.
   ○ a. in the natural world   ○ b. in hot weather
   ○ c. in a short time

7. **Shock waves** rocked the plane.
   ○ a. waves of air   ○ b. ocean waves   ○ c. surprising news

8. He was lucky to **regain** control of his plane.
   ○ a. remember   ○ b. share   ○ c. get again

9. A special plane was needed to **challenge** the sound barrier.
   ○ a. change   ○ b. build   ○ c. test

10. He **shattered** the sound barrier.
    ○ a. kept alive   ○ b. understood   ○ c. broke completely

Writing Your Ideas

■ Imagine that you are Chuck Yeager. On a separate sheet of paper, write a poem describing your feelings as you crash through the sound barrier.

Remembering What You Read

■ Answer the questions.

1. Name something bad that happened to Chuck Yeager during World War II. _____

_____

2. Why was the Bell X-1 built? _____

_____

3. How was the B-29 helpful in breaking the sound barrier? _____

_____

4. What happened to the shock waves when Chuck Yeager broke through the sound barrier? _____

_____

Building Skills—Use a Time Line

■ Use the time line to answer the questions.

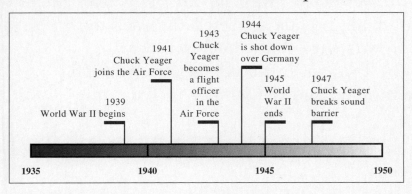

1. Did Chuck Yeager join the Air Force before or after World War II started? _____

2. In what year did Chuck Yeager become an Air Force flight officer? _____

3. Was World War II still going on when Chuck Yeager broke the sound barrier? _____

4. When was Chuck Yeager shot down over Germany? _____

TRUMAN'S WIN SHOCKS NATION

November 3, 1948—"DEWEY DEFEATS TRUMAN." This was the bold headline of the *Chicago Daily Tribune* late yesterday. The newspaper wanted to be the first to announce the new President of the United States. So the *Tribune* did not wait for all the votes to be counted. After all, no one expected the race to be close. Everyone was sure that Thomas Dewey would beat Harry S. Truman. But everyone was wrong! All the votes are in now. And the winner is Truman!

Completely Wrong

The people at the *Chicago Daily Tribune* were not the only ones to get it wrong. On November 1, *Life* magazine ran a picture of Thomas Dewey, "the next President," riding on a boat. *Billboard* also had Dewey on its November cover. The title was "Our Next President."

In September Elmo Roper of *Fortune* magazine took a **poll**. It showed Dewey ahead by 15 **percentage** points. This was such a huge lead that Roper ran no more polls. He felt Dewey had the **election** wrapped up.

John O'Donnell, a writer for the *New York Daily News*, was another person who had been sure Dewey would win. On November 3, he asked, "How is it possible to be so **utterly**, completely wrong?"

Truman holds up a copy of the *Chicago Daily Tribune*.

This young girl gave Truman a basket of flowers while he was campaigning for president.

Truman Against Dewey

Harry S. Truman was already serving as President of the United States when he entered the 1948 election. In 1944 he had become **Vice President** for Franklin Roosevelt. In 1945 Roosevelt died. Truman took over as President. Still, no one thought Truman could win an election on his own. Besides, Democrats had been in the White House since 1933. The country seemed ready for a change. Even top members of Truman's own Democratic party thought he would lose. They tried to find someone else to run. But no one wanted to run against Dewey. So the Democrats were left with Truman.

Thomas Dewey was the governor of New York. He had run for President in 1944 and lost to Roosevelt. In 1948 the Republican party picked him to run again. This time he was the **favorite**. Like everyone else, Dewey was sure he would win. "All I have to do," he thought, "is **avoid** making any mistakes." Dewey was very careful. He made the same safe speech over and over again.

Truman did not play it safe. He attacked Dewey hard. He said things that stirred up the voters. Truman also told people to forget the polls. "Polls are like sleeping pills," he said. "They are designed to **lull** the voters into sleeping on Election Day. But the people are not being fooled."

Election Day

On November 2, Dewey stayed up most of the night. He was all set to declare **victory**. He even had a speech ready. Truman went to bed early. "There's no reason to stay up," he said. "The results will not be known until tomorrow."

Again, Truman was right. The voting was very close in some key states. Early results showed Truman **edging** ahead. But the Republicans were not worried. They still thought their man would win. The next morning they learned they were wrong. Harry Truman had won. He had pulled off the biggest election surprise in American history. The voters had made it clear who the next president would be.

Harry Truman is sworn in as president after Franklin Roosevelt died.

73

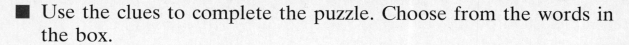

■ Use the clues to complete the puzzle. Choose from the words in the box.

victory
edging
avoid
election
vice president
utterly
poll
percentage
favorite
lull

Across

2. person who is liked the most

3. officer below president

6. totally

8. out of 100

9. gathering answers from many people

Down

1. stay away from

3. win

4. moving slowly

5. contest decided by voting

7. make sleepy

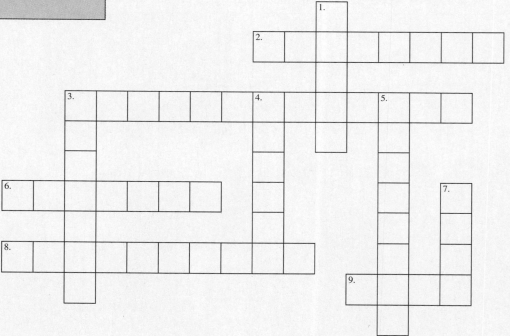

Writing Your Ideas

■ Imagine that you are Thomas Dewey. On a separate sheet of paper, describe your feelings when you learn the results of the election.

Remembering What You Read

■ Fill in the circle next to the best ending for each sentence.

1. Truman took over as President after the death of
   ○ a. Thomas Dewey.   ○ b. Franklin Roosevelt.
   ○ c. Elmo Roper.

2. In 1948 most people thought Thomas Dewey was going to
   ○ a. win.   ○ b. lose.   ○ c. drop out of the race.

3. Harry Truman gave speeches that
   ○ a. lulled people.   ○ b. stirred people up.
   ○ c. frightened people.

4. The winner of the 1948 election for president was
   ○ a. Harry Truman.   ○ Thomas Dewey.
   ○ c. John O'Donnell.

Thinking Critically—Main Ideas

■ Underline the two most important ideas from the story.

1. Harry Truman surprised people by winning the 1948 election.

2. Many people listened to speeches given by Thomas Dewey and Harry Truman.

3. Harry Truman believed in himself even when others didn't.

4. Thomas Dewey ran for president two times, but lost both times.

CINTRÓN FIGHTS BULL IN SPAIN

November 1, 1949—The people of Spain had never seen anything like it. They had watched many bullfighters leap around a ring with an angry bull. But the bullfighters had always been men. By law, women could face bulls only on horseback. Very few women chose even to do that. Then, last month, the law was broken. A woman bullfighter named Conchita Cintrón appeared in Jaén, Spain. As the crowd cheered, she got off her horse. Then she turned to face the charging bull.

Conchita Cintrón, at the age of 13, performs in Mexico before a crowd of 10,000.

A Taste for Drama

Conchita Cintrón was born in 1922 in Chile. One year later, her family moved to Peru. Cintrón began riding horses when she was very young. One day, the horse she was riding crashed into a fence. The animal rolled over on her twice. Cintrón was **bruised**, but also excited. "Until then riding had been a childish **attraction**," she later said. "But I had just had a taste of **drama** and I liked it."

Cintrón's riding teacher was Ruy da Camara. He had once been a bullfighter in Portugal, where fighters ride horses in the ring. Camara still loved bullfighting. He started to teach Cintrón about it. First he set up make-believe fights for her. A boy holding a chair played the bull. Cintrón learned to control her horse and hold a sword at the same time. Soon, she was ready for the real thing. Camara agreed to let her start fighting small bulls.

Make Way for Conchita!

At 13 years old, Cintrón was in her first bullfighting **exhibition**. She amazed everyone. People found it hard to believe that a girl so young could be so brave. Several years later, Cintrón went to Mexico. There she was given the chance to fight a large four-year-old bull. In the past, she had only fought small bulls. This bull would be far more dangerous. "This is my big chance," Cintrón thought.

Cintrón did a great job. She fought the huge bull with **grace** and courage. The fans loved her. Said one writer, "This little girl of 15 fights like an angel. Make way for Conchita!"

On Foot in Spain

Next, Cintrón learned to fight bulls on foot. This was how bullfighters in Spain did it. From age 15 to 28, she fought 400 bulls on foot. She also fought 800 bulls on horseback. Twice she was **gored** by a bull. Once she almost died.

Fifteen-year-old Cintrón greets the crowd as she enters the arena.

78

Cintrón poses with her fellow performers before a bullfight in France.

By 1949 Cintrón was a hero in South America. She was happy with her life. But one **goal** remained. She wanted to fight on foot in Spain. After all, Spain was the center of the bullfighting world. For years, she had **pleaded** with Spanish officials to let her do it. They refused. "If you get off your horse," they said, "it will be your last fight in Spain!"

In October 1949, Cintrón was in Spain for a fight on horseback. When she rode into the ring, fans cheered loudly. Suddenly, Cintrón jumped off her horse. With only her sword and her **cape**, she faced the bull on foot.

The bull **thundered** past the cape several times. Cintrón laid her sword on the ground. She did not want to kill this bull. Her dream had come true. At the age of 28, she was ready to give up bullfighting. As she left the ring, she had tears in her eyes. But Cintrón knew her name would always be part of bullfighting history.

Building Vocabulary

■ Match each word with its meaning.

_____ 1. gored

_____ 2. cape

_____ 3. bruised

_____ 4. attraction

_____ 5. grace

_____ 6. goal

a. cloth that hangs from the shoulders

b. something that catches a person's attention

c. showing beauty

d. something that a person hopes to get

e. stabbed by the horn of an animal

f. hit or bumped so that the skin shows a mark

Part B

■ Read each sentence. Fill in the circle next to the best meaning for the word in dark print. You may use the glossary.

1. Cintrón was in her first bullfighting **exhibition** at age 13.
   ○ a. accident   ○ b. show   ○ c. magazine

2. Cintrón liked the **drama** of bullfighting.
   ○ a. dream   ○ b. noise   ○ c. excitement

3. Cintrón **pleaded** with Spanish officials.
   ○ a. played   ○ b. became happy   ○ c. begged

4. The bull **thundered** toward Cintrón.
   ○ a. moved loudly   ○ b. growled loudly   ○ c. fell

Writing Your Ideas

■ Imagine you are Conchita Cintrón. On a separate sheet of paper, describe how you feel as you walk out of the ring for the last time.

Remembering What You Read

■ Some of the statements below are true. Others are false. Place a check in front of the three things that happened in the story.

_____ 1. Conchita Cintrón fought bulls on foot and on horseback.

_____ 2. Conchita Cintrón was a hero in South America.

_____ 3. Spanish officials begged Cintrón to fight a bull on foot.

_____ 4. Conchita Cintrón's last bullfight took place in Spain.

_____ 5. Conchita Cintrón was killed by a bull.

Building Skills—Read a Map

■ Use the map to answer the questions.

1. What country lies to the west of Spain?_____

2. Is Madrid closer to Toledo or Granada?_____

3. What two bodies of water border Spain?_____

_____

4. Name three cities found in Spain:_____

_____

ARMSTRONG TAKES PARIS BY STORM

November 4, 1949—Last night Louis Armstrong won over the city of Paris, France. His sweet horn had people tapping their feet. His deep singing voice had them clapping their hands. Armstrong had the crowd standing and cheering for more. He and his band played the latest and hottest American music. One song that really rocked the house was "Boogie-woogie on the St. Louis Blues."

Getting Started

Paris wasn't the only city to go wild over Armstrong's music. Fans around the world stood in line for hours to hear him. When there were no seats left, they willingly sat in the **aisles**. They cheered Armstrong at airports. Crowds shouted "Welcome, Louie!" when he stepped off a plane.

Louis Armstrong grew up loving music. At the age of five, he was already **performing**. He sang on the streets near his home in New Orleans, Louisiana. Armstrong's family had little money. So Armstrong played a guitar made from an old cigar box. Later he learned to play the trumpet. Often he did not use **sheet music**. He just made up the music as he went along.

Armstrong plays his trumpet for admirers in Paris, France.

Louis Armstrong was the most famous jazz trumpeter in the world.

At the age of 22, Armstrong moved to Chicago. By this time, he was an **accomplished** jazz musician. One day he was making a record. His sheet music fell to the floor. Armstrong did not stop singing to pick it up. He kept going. He couldn't remember the words to the song. So he started singing syllables that had no meaning. At that moment, Louis Armstrong invented "scat singing." Soon jazz singers everywhere were singing "scat."

Bringing Jazz to the World

In 1932, at the age of 32, Louis Armstrong made his first trip overseas. He was an **instant** hit. Everyone loved his style of American **jazz**. Over the next 40 years, Armstrong played in more than 100 countries.

In Hungary, over 91,000 fans came to one of his shows. In Italy, they lined the streets to get his **autograph**. In Africa, Armstrong was welcomed as a hero. In Leopoldville in the Congo, fans carried him on a throne to the stage. It seemed that Louis Armstrong was a headline story wherever he went.

Making It Up

Armstrong knew what the fans wanted to hear. They wanted to hear his trumpet. He carried it with him wherever he went. People also wanted to hear his singing. They loved to listen to him make up words and rhythms as he went along.

One day in 1949, Armstrong was in Rome, Italy. He was **sightseeing** at the Coliseum, the 2,000-year-old Roman **stadium**. Fans gathered to see Armstrong. He sat down on a stone wall. Thinking quickly, he made up a song and performed it for the crowd:

Sittin' on the stones of Rome
Make me wanna say I'm home
People everywhere
Stop and sit and stare
Make my trumpet want
    to **blare** . . .

Louis Armstrong was easily the most famous jazz trumpeter in the world. From Paris to Tokyo to New York, he filled people's lives with music. And he did it with the biggest smile in show business. He played and sang all the great jazz songs of the day. "You can't play anything on a horn," trumpeter Miles Davis said in the 1960s, "that Louis hasn't played."

Louis Armstrong jokes with reporters in 1957.

Building Vocabulary

■ Write the best word or words to complete each sentence. Use each word once.

---

aisles	performing	sheet music	accomplished	jazz
instant	sightseeing	stadium	blare	autograph

---

1. People sat in ——————— to hear Armstrong play.

2. The Coliseum is a 2,000-year-old ———————.

3. When Armstrong went overseas, he was an ——————— hit.

4. Armstrong was an ——————— musician.

5. Armstrong went ——————— in Rome.

6. Armstrong wanted to make his trumpet ———————.

7. Armstrong was famous for playing ———————.

8. Armstrong was ——————— at the age of five.

9. Armstrong dropped his ——————— ———————.

10. Many people wanted to get Armstrong's ———————.

Writing Your Ideas

■ Imagine you are Louis Armstrong. On a separate sheet of paper, write how it feels to be so famous.

Remembering What You Read

■ Answer the questions.

1. What type of music did Louis Armstrong play?_____

   _____

2. How did Armstrong invent "scat singing?"_____

   _____

3. What instrument did Armstrong play as an adult?_____

   _____

4. How did people in Europe treat Armstrong?_____

   _____

Thinking Critically—Sequence

■ Number the sentences to show the order in which things happened in the story. The first one is done for you.

____ Louis Armstrong visited the Coliseum in Rome.

____ Louis Armstrong made his first trip overseas.

____ Miles Davis said, "You can't play anything on a horn that Louis hasn't played."

____ Louis Armstrong invented scat singing.

_1_ Louis Armstrong played a guitar made from an old cigar box.

Glossary

accomplished, page 84
To be accomplished is to be very good at something.

achievement, page 37
An achievement is something worthwhile that you have done.

admiral, page 21
An admiral is a top officer in the navy.

aircraft carriers, page 21
Aircraft carriers are ships that carry airplanes across seas. Aircraft carriers have long decks where planes can take off or land.

aisles, page 83
Aisles are the walkways between rows of seats.

annex, page 56
An annex is a room that has been added on to a building.

arrested, page 42
To be arrested is to be picked up and held by the police.

athlete, page 47
An athlete is a person who plays sports well.

attraction, page 77
An attraction is something that catches a person's attention or draws a person toward it.

autograph, page 84
An autograph is a person's name written in his or her own handwriting.

avoid, page 72
To avoid means to stay away from.

banquet, page 30
A banquet is a large, fancy meal prepared for many people.

barrier, page 63
A barrier is something that blocks the way. The sound barrier is the speed that sound travels.

batting average, page 5
A batting average shows how often a batter gets a hit. Good batters have batting averages around .300, which is three hits out of ten times at bat.

blare, page 85
To blare is to make a loud noise.

bomber, page 21
A bomber is a plane that carries and drops bombs.

broadcasts, page 42
Broadcasts are programs that are sent out over the radio or TV.

bruised, page 77
To be bruised is to get a dark mark on your skin from being hit or bumped.

bunted, page 7
If a batter bunts, he just taps the ball with his bat so the ball goes only a short distance.

cape, page 79
A cape is a cloth that is worn around a person's shoulders.

challenge, page 65
To challenge is to test.

citizen, page 41
A citizen is a person who is part of a country. A citizen has the rights granted by that country.

college, page 35
College is a school of higher learning people may go to after high school.

concentration camps, page 55
Concentration camps are prisons where people are treated very badly.

condemn, page 57
To condemn means to decide that something is wrong or bad.

Congress, page 17
Congress is a group of people who make laws for the United States.

considerate, page 30
Considerate means thinking of other people's feelings.

contract, page 48
A contract is an agreement between two people or groups.

courage, page 50
Someone who has courage is brave.

courteous, page 30
Courteous means polite.

decent, page 29
Decent means meeting certain basic standards.

declare, page 17
To declare is to announce.

depressed, page 57
Depressed means to be sad, discouraged, and without hope.

discriminated, page 31
To be discriminated against is to be treated badly for some unfair reason, such as age or skin color.

donate, page 36
To donate is to give.

double plays, page 7
A double play means two outs are made on one play.

drama, page 77
Drama means excitement and adventure.

drill, page 16
A drill is a practice of some kind.

edging, page 73
Edging means moving slowly.

effort, page 29
Effort means working hard to do something. The war effort was the work that was done to fight the war.

election, page 71

An election is a contest where people choose a winner by voting.

embargo, page 13

An embargo is a decision by a government not to sell certain things to another country.

emergencies, page 36

An emergency is a dangerous event that calls for quick action.

engineers, page 63

Engineers are people who design new machines.

equipment, page 23

Equipment is the tools or supplies that are needed to do something.

evil, page 55

Evil means very bad and full of hate.

exhaustion, page 59

Exhaustion is when a person becomes very tired and weak.

exhibition, page 78

An exhibition is a show.

existed, page 64

To exist is to be real.

extremely, page 22

Extremely means very.

favorite, page 72

The favorite means the person who is liked the most.

fielding, page 48

Fielding means catching or picking up a ball that a batter has hit.

fuel, page 25

Fuel makes engines run.

gas chambers, page 55

Gas chambers are closed rooms where people are killed with poison gas.

goal, page 79

A goal is something that a person works to get.

gored, page 78

To be gored is to be wounded by the horn of an animal.

grace, page 78

Grace means showing beauty and style.

guilty, page 43

To be guilty means to have done something wrong.

high and outside, page 8

A pitch that is high and outside reaches the batter too high and too far away to be a strike.

homesick, page 30

To be homesick means to miss your home.

idiotic, page 57

Idiotic means foolish.

infamy, page 17
Infamy means being famous for some bad act.

influence, page 42
To influence is to use your power over someone to change his or her actions or feelings.

instant, page 84
Instant means right away.

insults, page 50
An insult is something that is said or done to hurt someone's feelings.

jazz, page 84
Jazz is a kind of music that was made famous in America. In jazz, the music can be changed by the musicians as they go along.

jockey, page 35
A jockey is a person who rides horses in races.

labor, page 29
Labor means work.

leads, page 49
A lead is when a runner moves off a base toward the next base before the pitcher pitches the ball.

lull, page 73
To lull is to make sleepy and calm.

minor league, page 47
A minor league is a group of baseball teams where players get ready for the major leagues.

mission, page 22
A mission is a special and important job.

officials, page 14
Officials are the people in charge.

orphan, page 42
An orphan is someone whose father and mother are dead.

pardoned, page 43
To be pardoned means that someone in power has forgiven you for your crime, and freed you from punishment.

percentage, page 71
Percentage means how many out of a group of 100. Fifteen percent means 15 out of 100.

performing, page 83
To perform is to put on a show for people.

physically, page 64
Physically means having to do with the natural world.

plasma, page 36
Plasma is the liquid part of blood.

pleaded, page 79
To plead is to beg.

poll, page 71
A poll is taken by asking a large number of people a question and then counting the different answers.

quarrel, page 57
A quarrel is an angry fight with words.

radar, page 15
Radar is a machine that uses radio waves to show where objects such as airplanes are.

reeling, page 21
To be reeling is to feel like you are spinning because you have been greatly surprised by something.

regain, page 64
To regain is to get again.

researchers, page 36
Researchers are people who study something carefully in order to learn about it.

rhythm, page 6
Rhythm means the timing or speed of some action.

risked, page 63
To risk is to take a chance of losing something.

rookie, page 51
A rookie is a player who is in his first season of play.

run-down, page 31
Run-down means in bad shape and ready to fall apart.

runways, page 21
Runways are long flat roads where planes take off or land.

scholarship, page 35
A scholarship is money given to a student to help pay for his or her schooling.

shattered, page 67
To be shattered is to be broken completely.

sheet music, page 83
Sheet music is music that is written on loose pieces of paper.

shock waves, page 64
Shock waves are strong waves of air.

shocked, page 17
To be shocked is to be very surprised and upset.

sightseeing, page 85
Sightseeing means visiting famous places or spots.

souvenir, page 9
A souvenir is something that a person keeps because it reminds him or her of something special.

stadium, page 85
A stadium is a building with rows of seats built around an open field.

streak, page 5
A streak is a period of time when something happens again and again. In baseball, a hitting streak is a large number of games in a row that a batter gets a hit.

strike, page 14
A strike is an attack against an enemy.

style, page 5
Style means showing beauty and skill.

succeed, page 48
To succeed means to do well.

system, page 36
A system is a planned way of doing something.

tense, page 57
Tense means nervous and worried.

threats, page 50
Threats are statements that something bad will be done to hurt or punish you.

thrown out, page 7
A runner is thrown out when the other team throws the ball to a base where the runner is headed, and it is caught before the runner arrives.

thundered, page 79
To thunder is to move heavily and loudly.

traitor, page 43
A traitor is a person who has turned against his or her own country and is helping the enemy.

transfusions, page 36
A transfusion takes blood from one person and puts it into another person.

treason, page 42
Treason means turning against your own country by helping an enemy.

trial, page 42
A trial is when someone is brought to court to see if he or she has broken a law.

utterly, page 71
Utterly means totally.

vice president, page 72
A vice president is the officer in charge after the president.

victory, page 73
A victory means a win.

volunteers, page 22
Volunteers are people who offer to help.

wages, page 29
Wages are money paid for work done.

walked, page 7
In baseball, a walk means the pitcher throws four bad pitches to a batter. This allows the batter to "walk" to first base.

warships, page 13
Warships are ships that are built to fight battles.

wound, page 63
A wound is the cutting or hurting of a body part.

Keeping Score

1. Count the number of correct answers you have for each activity.
2. Write these numbers in the boxes in the chart.
3. Ask your teacher to give you a score (maximum score 5) for Writing Your Ideas.
4. Add up the numbers to get a final score.

Stories	Building Vocabulary	Writing Your Ideas	Remembering What You Read	Building Skills	Thinking Critically	Score
DiMaggio Streak Ends						/22
Pearl Harbor Attacked!						/27
Doolittle Blasts Tokyo						/27
Lending a Helping Hand						/23
Blood Breakthrough						/23
Tokyo Rose Arrested!						/24
Jackie Robinson Joins Dodgers						/23
Tragic Story Told						/26
Sound Barrier Broken!						/23
Truman's Win Shocks Nation						/21
Cintrón Fights Bull in Spain						/22
Armstrong Takes Paris by Storm						/24

Answer Key

DiMaggio Streak Ends   Pages 4–11

Building Vocabulary
Part A: 1-f, 2-a, 3-b, 4-c, 5-d, 6-e
Part B: 1. batting average, 2. streak,
3. high and outside, 4. souvenir

Writing Your Ideas Answers will vary.

Remembering What You Read
3, 5, 6

Building Skills—Read a Table
1. 1940   2. 1939, 1940, 1941
3. 193   4. 30

Pearl Harbor Attacked! Pages 12–19

Building Vocabulary
1-a, 2-c, 3-b, 4-b, 5-a, 6-c, 7-c, 8-b, 9-b, 10-b

Writing Your Ideas Answers will vary.

Remembering What You Read
1-b, 2-b, 3-c, 4-b

Thinking Critically—Fact or Opinion
1-O, 2-O, 3-F, 4-O, 5-F, 6-O, 7-F, 8-F

Doolittle Blasts Tokyo   Pages 20–27

Building Vocabulary
Across: 2. mission, 4. bomber, 6. aircraft carriers, 9. runways, 10. fuel
Down: 1. volunteers, 3. equipment,
5. extremely, 7. admiral, 8. reeling

Writing Your Ideas Answers will vary.

Remembering What You Read
1. Jimmy Doolittle led it.
2. The runways were very short.
3. The planes needed to be lighter so they could take off on short runways.
4. They headed for China.

Building Skills—Read a Graph
1. the American Revolution
2. World War II
3. More died in battle during the Civil War.
4. yes

Lending a Helping Hand Pages 28–33

Building Vocabulary
1. considerate, 2. Labor, 3. run-down,
4. effort, 5. discriminated, 6. decent,
7. homesick, 8. banquet, 9. wages
10. courteous

Writing Your Ideas Answers will vary.

Remembering What You Read
2, 3, 4

Thinking Critically—Cause and Effect
1. many Americans were overseas fighting World War II.
2. they could get better jobs in America.
3. they wanted to make Mexican workers feel at home.
4. many houses were too run-down to live in.
5. Mexico, too, had declared war on Germany and Japan.

Blood Breakthrough   Pages 34–39

Building Vocabulary
1-i, 2-a, 3-h, 4-b, 5-c, 6-d, 7-g, 8-e, 9-f, 10-j

Writing Your Ideas Answers will vary.

Remembering What You Read
1-a, 2-b, 3-a, 4-b

Building Skills—Use a Diagram
1. It travels to the left side of the heart.
2. It goes to the body parts—head, arms, legs.
3. The right side sends blood to the lungs.
4. The two sides are the left side and the right side.

Tokyo Rose Arrested   Pages 40–45

Building Skills
Part A: 1. broadcasts, 2. treason, 3. guilty,
4. pardoned
Part B: 1-f, 2-a, 3-c, 4-b, 5-d, 6-e

Writing Your Ideas Answers will vary.

Remembering What You Read
1. She went to visit a sick aunt.
2. They tried to make soldiers homesick.
3. They thought she was funny.
4. She was arrested and spent 6 1/2 years in prison.

Thinking Critically—Sequence
5, 1, 3, 4, 2

Jackie Robinson Joins Dodgers!   Pages 46–53

Building Vocabulary
Across: 2. insults, 7. rookie, 8. athlete,

9. succeed, 10. leads

Down: 1. minor league, 3. threats, 4. contracts, 5. fielding, 6. courage

Writing Your Ideas Answers will vary.

Remembering What You Read
1-b, 2-a, 3-c, 4-b

Building Skills—Use a Time Line
1. 1956
2. no
3. 1919
4. He was elected to the Baseball Hall of Fame.

Tragic Story Told   Pages 54–61

Building Vocabulary
1. idiotic, 2. annex, 3. concentration camps, 4. quarrel, 5. tense, 6. exhaustion, 7. gas chambers, 8. evil, 9. condemn 10. depressed

Writing Your Ideas Answers will vary.

Remembering What You Read
1, 3, 4

Thinking Critically—Conclusions
1. they were Jews.
2. they wanted to get away from the Nazis.
3. they were afraid the Nazis would capture them.
4. the Nazis took her to a concentration camp.
5. he hoped to find his family there.

Sound Barrier Broken!   Pages 62–69

Building Vocabulary
1-b, 2-a, 3-b, 4-b, 5-c, 6-a, 7-a, 8-c, 9-c, 10-c

Writing Your Ideas Answers will vary.

Remembering What You Read
1. His plane was shot down./He was wounded in the leg./He was jailed by Spanish police.
2. It was built to test the sound barrier.
3. It carried the Bell X-1 into the air.
4. The shock waves disappeared.

Building Skills—Use a Time Line
1. after
2. 1943
3. no
4. 1944

Truman's Win Shocks Nation   Pages 70–75

Building Vocabulary
Across: 2. favorite, 3. vice president, 6. utterly, 8. percentage, 9. poll
Down: 1. avoid, 3. victory, 4. edging, 5. election, 7. lull

Writing Your Ideas Answers will vary.

Remembering What You Read
1-b, 2-a, 3-b, 4-a

Thinking Critically—Main Ideas
1, 3

Cintrón Fights Bull in Spain   Pages 76–81

Building Vocabulary
Part A: 1-e, 2-a, 3-f, 4-b, 5-c, 6-d
Part B: 1-b, 2-c, 3-c, 4-a

Writing Your Ideas Answers will vary.

Remembering What You Read
1, 2, 4

Building Skills—Read a Map:
1. Portugal
2. Madrid is closer to Toledo.
3. The Atlantic Ocean and the Mediterranean Sea
4. Answers should include three of the following: Barcelona, Granada, Madrid, Pomplona, Santiago, Toledo

Armstrong Takes Paris by Storm   Pages 82–87

Building Vocabulary
1. aisles, 2. stadium, 3. instant, 4. accomplished, 5. sightseeing, 6. blare, 7. jazz, 8. performing, 9. sheet music 10. autograph

Writing Your Ideas Answers will vary.

Remembering What You Read
1. He played jazz.
2. He began singing nonsense words after dropping his sheet music.
3. He played the trumpet.
4. They treated him like a hero.

Thinking Critically—Sequence
4, 3, 5, 2, 1